DE LORES MAY RICHARDS

MUSIC FROM MY

HEART

55 ORIGINAL SONGS

1955-2020

ACKNOWLEDGMENT

This book is dedicated to my family for their assistance

and their patience during the 2020 Covid-19 drama.

This contributed to the success of this book.

Thanks to: Ken Richards and our children,

Sherry, David, Lori, and Diana and their families.

TABLE OF CONTENTS

MY HEART'S A MARCHING FOOL

When I look at this song, I laugh. In 1955, I was traveling in an all-girl band called "Ann Jones and her Western sweethearts". We were all over the western states in bars and dance halls. We also went to Japan, and Korea. Canada and Mexico. I was 19 years old. I learned so much about playing songs "by ear" instead of reading the music that I had been taught.

One night, in Carlsbad NM, I met a young man who was at the dance with a buddy. I was in the mood for a career in music—I did not realize that this was going to be someone that I would spend my life with. My life up to that time was play music, ride the van all night long, and play music at night again. I had no desire to have a husband or tie my life down with a bunch of kids.

I should have known that God brought me to that town and brought Ken also to that town with a plan. All We had to do is see the wisdom in that plan. I immediately fell in love with this young man that loved music as I did, and we courted mostly by mail. We were married in 1956 and, of course, I gave up traveling. We started out our married life playing music together.

This silly song was written before we tied the knot and was my first song as an adult. Please note. There is a world of difference between the first and the last song in this book.

SO I SMILE!

MY HEARTS A MARCHING FOOL

WRITTEN 1955

DeLores Richards

LADYBUG

I learned a nursery rhyme when I was a child. I didn't know the meaning, but we sang it often.

"Lady bug, Lady bug, fly away home.

Your house is on fire, and your children are gone.

All but one and her name is Ann and she crept under the pudding pan."

There are many myths. One was that the ladybug represented godless worship in a time when Christianity was coming into popularity. The house referred to as burning referred to the destruction of pagan temples. Ann, the one who was saved, referred to those that escaped by going underground.

So, this is the inspiration for my "Ladybug "song. It easily turned into an unfaithful wife (or husband) who abandoned family for "one hour of bliss."

LADYBUG
(Written 1960)

DeLores Richards

You   may think your   new love is   worth more than   gold. You'll
You'll hurt all your   child - ren, you'll   burn them with   fire. They'll

lose all your   child-ren and   love will gr ow cold. And   where is   the
be oh, so   lone - ly to   suit your de -si - re. And   then you will

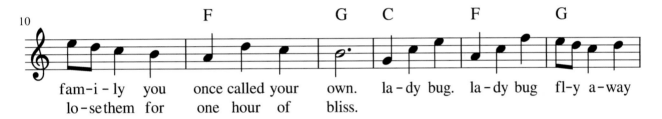

fam-i - ly you   once called your   own. la - dy bug. la - dy bug fl-y a-way
lo - se them for   one hour of   bliss.

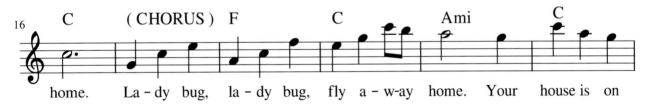

home. La - dy bug, la - dy bug, fly a - w-ay home. Your   house is on

fi - r - e your child-ren wi - ll burn. La - dy bug, La - dy bug fly a - wa-y

home. Go   back to your   love-d ones and   nev - er mo-re roam

THIS LIFE IS MINE

When I was going through the teenage years, I made the determination that I was not able to love anyone. Although I was raised going to a church, the teenage years seemed to have a void for me in that regard.

Teenagers often feel that they are alone. I was no different than all teenagers, but I thought I was. I prayed "God teach me how to Love". It was a simple prayer addressed to Him. I had not developed that much of a bond or relationship. I thought I did not know how to love. I was beginning to determine for myself what my life would be.
WAS I TO BE SURPRIZED!

In 1964, during the year of the birth of our fourth child, I looked back at my life and realized that God was answering my teenage prayer. He was teaching me through experience. It was not fast. It was not instant. It was up to me because He had given me this life. This life is mine.

This is what we had in store from God in just a few years-1974

THIS LIFE IS MINE
(Written 1964)

DeLores Richards

C   Ami   Dmi   G   C

Oh, Lord, this life is mine. You gave this life to me, babe full of hope, a

6   Dmi   G   C   Ami   Dmi

hard-fast mem - o - ry. You made this world my own and placed me all a

12   G   C   Dmi   G   C   C7

lone, but nev - er - less I found you con - stant - ly. I

17   F   Emi   F   C   F

jour-neyed all thru life and (I be-came a wife). a group of bab - ies
                    (then I took a wife)

22   G   C   C7   F   Emi   F   C

placed up-on my knee. But, time it hurr-ies on and soon the child-ren gone, the

29   F   Dmi   G   G7   C   Ami

one I loved had passed a-way from me. And, now, a-alone, I know that

35   Dmi   G   C   Dmi   G   C

soon I am to go. I thank you Lord for all you gave to me.

WATCH THE TIME GO BY

Some people have relatives who seem to have no goals in life and just kind of sit there and take life in. Of course, we too had an Uncle Bertie who did not accomplish anything in this life. He was smart even though he, like most people in the 1920's, did not receive much of an education. He did not desire such things. My Mom's siblings were raised on a houseboat. They were a fishing family. I remember how the brothers (when they were grown) would bring all kinds of fish to us. Sturgeon was our favorite fish. It is hardly available today.

Bertie worked sometime. I remember him living in a smelly little trailer with his 20's little green truck parked there by the Columbia River. He would visit my Mom and Larry, my stepdad, when I was a teen. He always argued with Larry. His blue eyes would continually blink as he sat in a chair almost flat on his back and smoked. The arguments, political, religious, etc, would continue for many hours.

As Bertie grew older, he worked less. He always said he would work only long enough in a year so that he would not pay taxes. Yet he collected disability in a regular fashion or anything else he could from the government.

He lived to an old age in a nursing home paid for by the government. He had no wife or children. And, as far as I know, he had no regrets for the way he lived his life.

MY MOTHER PAID FOR HIS FUNERAL

WHEN WE MOVED INTO THE CLATSKANIE HOUSE, WE FOUND THIS ANTIQUE PICKUP TOY THAT LOOKED LIKE THE 1920'S TRUCK THAT HE HAD.

WATCH THE TIME GO BY
(Written 1969)

DeLores Richards

POOR LITTLE RICH GIRL

In 1936 Shirley Temple starred in a movie called "Poor Little Rich Girl". In 1965, Andy Warhol filmed an underground remake to begin a series about the poor little rich girl. It did not develop into anything.

Was this on my mind in 1970? My mother took us to every Shirley Temple movie that was produced. She did not drive. We lived on Columbia Way in Longview, Washington. We were a few miles from town. That street is now called Industrial. Way. It was changed in the early 50's. All the houses were bought up in order to make way for an impending industrial site. All my Dad's siblings and my Mom's siblings had built houses and moved onto Columbia way to follow the 30's development of paper mills.

We walked to the rear of our two lots to the railway track. We followed the track to California Way and then to town. We walked to the Roxy theater. The cost of a theater ticket was only a quarter---and popcorn was cheaper. Then we took a visit to the local drugstore to get a big, creamy chocolate shake before we walked back home.

Back to the story: It could have been the movies, but my Mom spent a lot of time talking to us. Later she told us those stories. She said that I informed her, when I was just a toddler, that I was raised up in a rich family in my previous life. I was given everything and never had to do anything for myself. When I came into Mother's" life, I wanted to work for what I received. Whether that was true or not, I do not know. I did work and received more than I ever had imagined.
I'M 85 YEARS OLD AND LABORING STILL!

Poor Little

Rich Girl

Never to know
true love

POOR LITTLE RICH GIRL (Written 1970)

DeLores Richards

The word "Reborn" signifies a great event, whether it is the budding of a flower, or the acorn growing into a great Oak or even the beginning of a great new day. God has given us this earth to care for and the expectation is that we will do it well. He cares for us. The examples that we see daily are also applicable to human life. Made in the imagine of God, we enjoy rebirth at it's greatest. When man gets down, when he realizes that he needs the help of a greater power, when things get too great to bear, God is there. He has provided a new way to approach life. He will let us do what we want. We can decide to go "the new way" or we can flounder around on our own without even knowing His help is available.

In 1962, then with 3 of our 4 children, we came to this spot in our life. We studied the Bible and we came to conclusion that our life needed something. When we Discovered that God had given us a plan through Christ, we went into the waters of baptism, changed our lives, and went into the door of His kingdom. We have never regretted that!

REBORN
(Written 1970)

DeLores Richards

MY HOME IS NOT THIS LAND

"This land I love so very well."

Yes, I did love the beauties of this earth. In 1970 we were involved in raising our children. We were living on the Clataskanie Oregon hill. We were playing music. The little one was on the drums. We liked Herb Alpert music. The three oldest had music classes. We had a dog named Holstein who crooned out the notes that Lori Ann would play on her trumpet. We raised cattle and pigs and chickens. I spent time in the woods while the kids were in school. I picked berries. I made pies and fresh bread—and I wrote a few songs.

We were quite active with the kids in the Church. This was a major part of our lives. Regarding the spiritual aspects of this song, my viewpoint was quite different than now. I believed in a heaven not available till death. My songs changed over the years. We now realize that God's kingdom is accessible. Jesus opened the gate for us. Living in the kingdom, we realize things are not always so nice here. But—we are set apart. If we look for the good, we will find it. This one thing can change the world. Our God is the "God of the living." So, amid the Covid-19 and the protests of 2020, we pray that the world will be a better world thru Him!

I still love the beauties of this earth!

MY HOME IS NOT THIS LAND
(Written 1970)

DeLores Richards

I CAN HEAR MY LORD

As time went by, I developed more of an understanding of the works of God. We cannot see or hear God, but we can comprehend his presence in our lives every day. We see all the signs of his activity. We hear things moving and growing. God has given every living creature the breath of life. They praise Him with their song. Should we do less?

Such pictures of birds on the telephone lines has always impressed me. As I look out my window towards the street, I see them. The lines, to me, represent the treble clef in my music books. Every little bird, to me, represents a note. I have often played their song in my heart. They are joining in the works of man to praise their God.

Watch for them!

(Photo- Joe Lavigne)

I CAN HEAR MY LORD
(Written 1971)

DeLores Richards

JESUS MY SAVIOR, MY OWN

This represents the type of traditional old songs that we sang at every service. Feelings that most of us have at times are quite apparent in them. We sang them, knew them by heart. We hummed them in the shower or in our daily work.

Likewise, my song has the same qualities. I am weak in myself. I require the need of a Savior to lift me up to the heights of glory--to be with him in his sweet home. And, in accepting that help, I am in Jesus-my Savior-my own.

"LIFTING MY SOUL TO THE HEIGHT OF IT'S DAY"

JESUS, MY SAVIOR, MY OWN
(Written 1971)

DeLores Richards

Of all the things that I have done, lift-ing my soul is
I can not of my own be strong, ev-en by works, I'm
Lift-ing my soul, I'm part of him ev-en if weak or

not the one. Do-ing the works that mean most to me
still not strong. Who takes the bur-den a-way from me
vis-ion dim, Still He can place me in His sweet home.

still does not set me free. He takes the sin and the
and can my soul un-bind?
Jes-us my sav-ior my own.

veil far a-way lift-ing my soul to the height of it's day, plac-ing it

where it does be-long, In Jes-us my sav-ior, my own.

THE THREE

My first instrumental song

In the pages to follow, you will find more instrumental songs of all sorts. Why did I call this "The Three?"

 It has a pattern of three notes together and that is the only reason for the title. It's peppy. It's fun. It is something I love to play. At this time, I was still playing the accordion. As the years went by, and as I became older, I went back to the piano or—as we call it now—the keyboard. It fits in a bag less than three feet long and you can carry it with one hand anywhere.

THE THREE
(Written 1972)

DeLores Richards

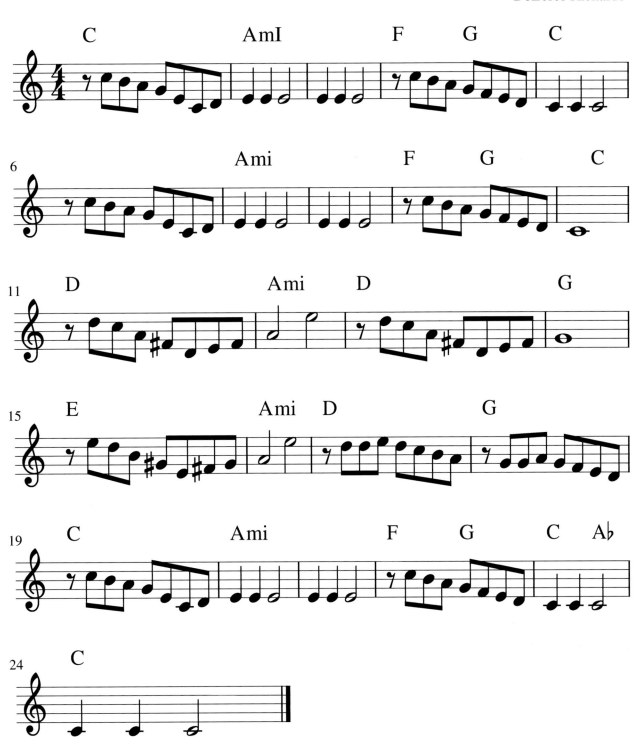

GRANDMOTHER PEARL

She was petite and delicate. Her unique maiden name was Pearl Ivy Rose. I wrote this song in memory of her.

In the 1940's, she made our little dolls hand sewn dresses with beautiful strips of material-- little hats and little shoes. We enjoyed those for years until we got too big to play with dolls. I wish I had kept some of them. This was years before Barbies.

Grandma raised 4 boys and my Mother. I have been told things about her family. Mother said that the oldest boy was her Dad's, but not her mother's. She stated also that many times her mom told her that she was not hers. It is a mystery that has never been solved. I have little locks of hair from the boys that my grandmother kept. DNA anyone?

In her older years, Grandma Pearl would seclude herself with her cats. She would run away often. She walked fast. I remember my Mother would have to chase her down and bring her back. She was quite sickly in those years from neglecting her health. Nothing was known about Alzheimer's. Looking back at her mental state, I can see it as a possibility. Grandma Pearl met Sherry, but after that time she wanted nothing to do with great grandchildren.

We were close to grandma when we were children. We visited often. Columbia way in Longview Washington was populated with my Dad's brothers and my Mother's brothers. All the families were within a couple of blocks. Thank you, Grandmother Pearl, for being you!

1940. I am showing off my doll with her new clothes made by grandma

GRANDMOTHER PEARL
(Written 1974)

DeLores Richards

A DAUGHTER'S LAMENT

Going back again- to the childhood, I fell in love with my Dad. Girls often fall in love with the Dad in the family—the big strong man that protects them and cares for them. I was no different. Dad wanted boys, but it was not to be. So, I was the one that he taught how to hammer and nail. I was the one that helped him build the garage.

Dad took us girls fishing. We'd get the fish nets out and the whole family went smelt dipping on the Cowliz River. We would put our nets in and with the help of our strong Dad, we would pull out a whole net full of little silver fish. They were good fried. My Dad would put them in his smoker and they would be heaven itself—chewy and crispy.

We had trips to Mt St Helens. We climbed the mountain as little girls. We looked down into the deep clear "bottomless" Silver Lake. We visited Harry Truman at the little store. As I visit it now, it is gone. The mountain is a shell of itself. Silver Lake is no more. Everything was destroyed by ash in 1980. I saw the results from an airplane in July of 1980. Our childhood memory subjects often disappear like a mist of air—gone!

I have so many memories of my Dad until he and my Mom divorced when I was 13. It was a new life for us girls.

A DAUGHTER'S LAMENT'
Written 1974

DeLores Richards

Of - ten I have tak - en hi - m by the hand, tried to tell him
I will tempt this man with all my lov - ing ways, hold him close and
Then I told my moth - er all a - bout my dreams, how I want - ed

just the way I feel. But, he tos - ses out the win - dow all my dreams,
whis - per, "I love you." Wait for him to give me just a bit of praise.
much to mar - ry him. But, she told me that I was a bit too young,

try - ing to pre - tend that they're not real. In this girl - ish
There's so much I know that I can do. Though he says he
that my brok - en heart would have to mend. "In this big wide

heart of mine, lies a great new plan. It's to have his lov - ing
has a love, he will soon re - gret. He will turn a - way from
won - drous world, there are rules so sad. And, you can - not mar - ry

heart here with - in my hand.
her and will soon for - get.
him 'cause he is your Dad."

SHADOW ON THE WALL

Where did I find the inspiration for this song? We are the products of our previous experiences even when we do not realize it. Everything is in our memory. With research, I found there was a movie by that name in 1950. It starred Ann Southern, Zachery Scott, Giggi Perreau and Nancy Reagan. I no doubt saw it. I will again. The shadow aspect was throughout the movie, but my song dwells on the wrongly convicted person who was imprisoned. And I approached it as if he were guilty of that crime. Shadows were in his prison cell. Shadows were a sign that he would not ever see the outside again.

Nancy Reagan went on to be first lady of the white house in the 1980's.

SHADOW ON THE WALL
(Written 1974- revised 2020)

DeLores Richards

"you're the fair-est of the lad-ies that I talk to in my dreams each
Con-fined with-in those walls of gray, he saw sky thru bars of steel and

time I see your shad-ow on the wall.
en-vied ones that he would nev-er know.
It pas-ses thru this
His heart was low and

room of mine, I see it ev-ery day and then my heart is emp-ty all in
ten-der as re-pent-ing of his deeds. The joys of life, he knew would ne-ver

all. And, then I know the lon-i-ness of dream-ing emp-ty dreams. Yet,
flow. Re-mem-ber-ing the ma-ny just the same as he saw now. He

you will nev-er know this moan-ful call. And, still my heart is burn-ing, and
count-ed them as dust be-neath his feet. And, now he has no ten-der hand

still my heart is yearn-ing each time I see your shad-ow on the wall."
to touch him in his need. He on-ly sees the shad-ow on the wall.

1974

What happened in 1974 that made me so unable to pick a title for this song? The 70's mark a decade where our family was playing at the fairs and the granges. It marked a time also when the kids were growing up and making their own ways. Three were teenagers and would leave the nest Within a few years

This picture was taken in 1970. In 1975 David (in the background with his trombone) was deathly sick. His life was saved, but he lost his hearing and has had to deal with that his whole life

1974
(Written 1974)

DeLores Richards

LITTLE MISS CHATTERBOX

Diana has "LOST HER VOICE" with Grand Uncle Sidney Cathey in Lubbock Texas when she was just a small one.

However, she soon found it. It didn't go very far.

Then she could not stop talking.

LITTLE MISS CHATTERBOX

(Written 1974)

DeLores Richards

NOW: At the grand age of 85, I have learned much. The fulfilled dream is somewhat like this picture. It's all of us walking on the seashore with the power of God ever before us on this earth. It's giving him power to guide our steps and to enjoy life here to the fullest.

So when the end of our life does come, we know He still directs our steps always upward and to Him.

THIS IS MY DREAM

THEN:

I have a dreamy look as I think of this song I wrote in 1974. It's no longer the same dream as what I had then. My "dream" song was a prediction of the end of my life. Where the thought came from is beyond me. It shows that I had to wait until my death to enjoy the gifts of paradise. It means that at age 40, we do have thoughts of such things. They are based on what we know at that time. HOW COULD I HAVE BEEN SO WRONG?

THIS IS MY DREAM
(Written as late as 1974)

DeLores Richards

I'm but a pil - grim on this earth. I'm but a strang - er seek - ing birth, a birth of

life for - ev - er more. This is my dream. I know that He has gone be-

fore to op - en up the gold - en door. He has the pow - er in his hands, This is my dream.

All of my loved ones are here to be with me till the end. And I look

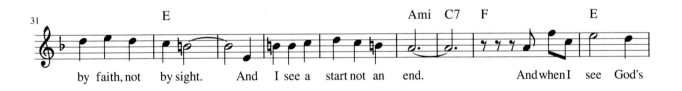

by faith, not by sight. And I see a start not an end. And when I see God's

shin - ing face, I know I've found the Mast - er's grace. The gift of God for - ev - er more,. e - ter - nal

life. (fade out)

ANOTHER BROKEN HEART TO MEND

This song is about a fellow who was unfaithful to his sweetheart. His wandering eye broke many a young lady's heart. I see this even today. It is a problem that society faces. However, in the end, he faces his own kind of sorrow when he falls in love with a girl with the same mindset as himself.

It's a "reap what you sow" story!

(photograph by Roman Kraft)

ANOTHER BROKEN HEART TO MEND
(Written 1975/77)

DeLores Richards

No mat-ter who they are, you leave them con - stant - ly. Your love you can not

share. For them you can not care. I see the fut-ure now my love.

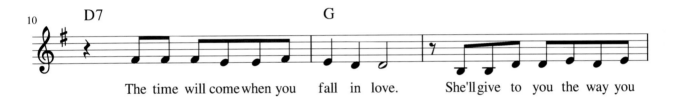

The time will come when you fall in love. She'll give to you the way you

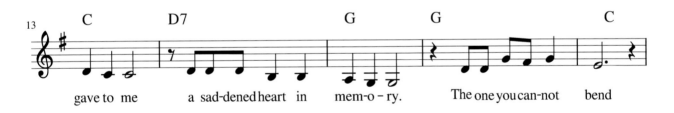

gave to me a sad-dened heart in mem-o - ry. The one you can-not bend

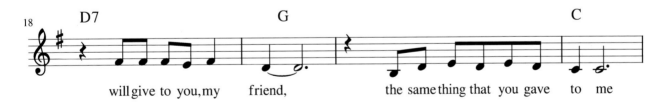

will give to you, my friend, the same thing that you gave to me

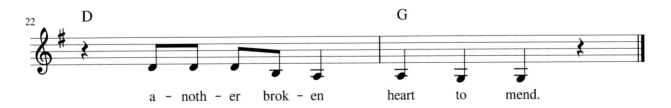

a - noth - er brok - en heart to mend.

IN A LITTLE WHILE

This must be the same fellow we saw in the last song.

This time he likes the girl enough to come back to her again and again. He apparently married her but can't seem to keep his vows. And---she so patiently just waits for the fellow to return. "In a little while" is a continuous thing in her life. She always has one eye on her watch and one eye on the door. It happens often to many.

IN A LITTLE WHILE
(Written 1975)

DeLores Richards

HE SANG SO SWEETLY

This is us through life. Ken has the most beautiful voice. I treasure those moments when he looks me directly in the eyes and sings out his love for me.

HE SANG SO SWEETLY
(Written 1975)

DeLores Richards

He sang so sweet-ly as he held my hand. Lit-tle did I know. (instrumental)

He sang so sweet-ly as he placed the band. This is when I know.

(instrumental) Mo-ments of si lence they came at the start. Mo-ments of

si lence came to our one heart. (instrumental) He sings so sweet-ly as

he holds my hand, sing-ing soft and low. (instrumental) He sings so

sweet-ly as he holds my hand. Now thru life we'll go. (INSTRUMENTAL)

STEP BY STEP

Take into consideration the many steps that we have taken over our lifetimes.

Then consider how many steps we are taking to get to where we are going.

Then consider why we are taking those steps.

What do we want to accomplish?

Then we should know what life is about.

(PHOTO BY CHAD-GREITER)

STEP BY STEP NEW SONG
(Written June 1977)

DeLores Richards

"THY PEOPLE SHALL BE MY PEOPLE"

Marriage is a gift from God. Two people are put into each other's lives. They are now one person. The poetry in the Book of Ruth has been used over and over to explain the love that one person has for another when coming together in unity. It has been used as a love story although it originally was used to proclaim Ruth's faithfulness to her mother-in-law and her God. It proclaims the same in the vows toward each other in the marriage relationship. We watched our four children grow and determine their own lives and we stood by and applauded their newfound freedoms. This song was written for one of our girls as she made her decision to come to the alter.

THY PEOPLE SHALL BE MY PEOPLE
(Written 1977)

THE STORY OF RUTH

DeLores Richards

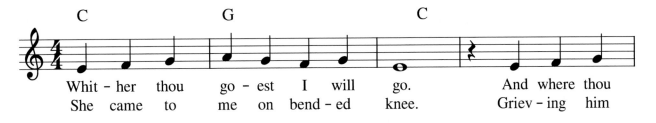

Whit - her thou go - est I will go. And where thou
She came to me on bend - ed knee. Griev - ing him

lodg - est I will lodge. Thy peo - ple will be my peo - ple
in hu - mil - i - ty. She said "My hus - band's gone and thy

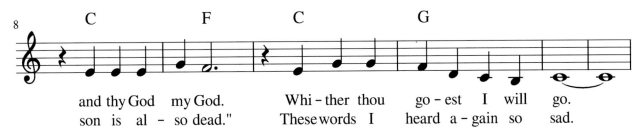

and thy God my God. Whi - ther thou go - est I will go.
son is al - so dead." These words I heard a - gain so sad.

And where thou di - est, I will die. There I will be bur - ied.
And where thou di - est I will die. There I will be bur - ied.

The Lord do so to me and more al - so, if ought but death part thee and
The Lord do so to me and more al - so, if ought but death part thee and

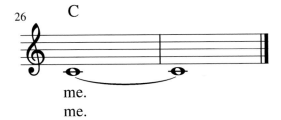

me.
me.

CATCH ME IN THE WIND

(Photo by Jennifer Krisztina Szauer)

When I was a little girl, I dreamt of flying. I looked at the birds and saw that they caught the wind. They soared above the treetops and looked down on us in a superior way. They were truly free! Do we ever lose our childhood dreams? Do we carry them thru life? I would still like to spread my wings and catch the wind!

CATCH ME IN THE WIND
(Written February 10, 1977)

DeLores Richards

TAKE ME BACK

Have you ever wanted to go back and live again the things that happened in your life? Have you wanted to go back to a most wonderful experience? Do you roll down the pictures on your cell phone or go back further and look at the old photograph albums? I think we all do! We remember those good things and push to the back of our minds those things we would change. We build our present lives on the things that happened to us in the past. We can't go back. God has given us these great lives, but we have to remember that this life is a learning experience and we need to appreciate it for what it is.

TAKE ME BAC K

(Written June 1977- revised 2020)

DeLores Richards

SHARE THE WORLD

Can one person make a difference?

It's a question we consider often.

I'm just one person. How can I help to correct this big mess of a world? Note the picture-a group of uke players donating their time to spread their light to others in an assisted living home for seniors. We can do our part. Don't lose heart. WE ARE MANY!

SHERRY

SHARE THE WORLD
(Written 1977)

DeLores Richards

HIS EVERLASTING THRONE

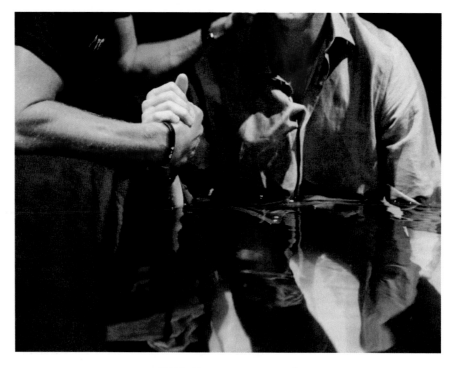

(PHOTO BY KELEB TAPP)

Bernie was baptized by Ken when we lived in Clatskanie Oregon. We often wonder where he is and if the experience changed his life forever like it did ours.

We lose tract of our friends over the years. Are they still with us?

Sometimes our relatives and friends leave this physical life, but we always remember what they meant to us and the memories are always there with us.

HIS EVERLASTING THRONE
(Written September 28th, 1977 at 9:45 pm)
(Bernie Abella's Baptism)

DeLores Richards

PLAY THAT SONG AGAIN FOR ME

As our family band gets bigger, I look back to 1977 when I wrote this song for our children to play. So much has happened. I could not have imagined that 43 years later, we would have this kind of wonderful communication with our family thru instruments and vocals. And, it will continue down thru their generations.

We now have small ones learning how to sing. They are belting out their own songs with confidence and talent. Thank God!

I repeat to my family "Play that song again for me!"

After Covid-19, of course.

PLAY THAT SONG AGAIN FOR ME
(Written February 1977)

DeLores Richards

THE OCEAN'S MY FRIEND

1978 was a time when our young ones were leaving the nest. Two were off on their own by this time—school, marriages, and so forth. It happened like it does in every family. I had more time to make friends with the ocean. It was a big, beautiful ocean where you could walk barefoot and dig your toes into the sand. You could lose all your cares in the ocean. I wrote this song about a drifter who made the ocean his friend. Through all his problems, through all his drifting, he could always come back to the ocean. It was his friend-his only friend.

THE OCEAN'S MY FRIEND
(Written 1978)

DeLores Richards

I KNOW THERE'S A GOD OUT THERE

IN 1979, I THOUGHT ABOUT THIS SERIOUSLY AND WROTE THIS SONG. I SAW HIM AS A KIND OF A DISTANT GOD. HE WALKED WITH ME BUT WASN'T QUITE HERE. HE WAS <u>OUT THERE!</u> HE WAS MUCH LIKE THE SEA FROM AFAR. I COULD SEE IT BUT NEVER QUITE PRECEIVE IT'S ENTIRE PRESENCE.

MANY YEARS LATER I DO SEE HIS EFFECT IN EVERYTHING FROM THE SMALLEST LIVING THING IN THE OCEAN TO THE LARGEST ANIMAL LIVING. HE'S IN THE WIND AND THE SEA.HE IS EVERYWHERE. HE IS IN MAN HIMSELF AND I SEE THIS EVERY DAY. <u>HE IS HERE WITH US!</u>

I KNOW THERE'S A GOD OUT THERE
(Written 1979)

DeLores Richards

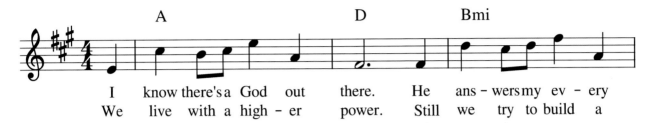

I know there's a God out there. He ans - wers my ev - ery
We live with a high - er power. Still we try to build a

prayer. And He walks with me a long the way of
tower. And we try to reach Him high a - bove, but

this old world and so I say Come take this walk with me and
He is here to guide with love. Come take this walk with me and

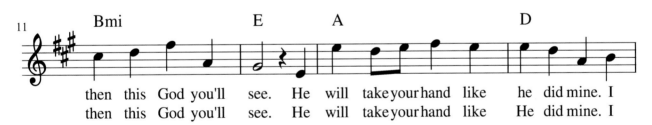

then this God you'll see. He will take your hand like he did mine. I
then this God you'll see. He will take your hand like He did mine. I

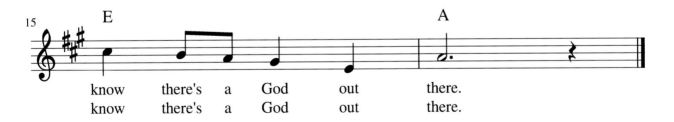

know there's a God out there.
know there's a God out there.

THIS?

OR

HOW DO WE KNOW WHAT THE GARDEN LOOKS LIKE?

THIS ?

OR THIS?

2012/01/19 21:58

HEAVENLY GARDEN OF GOD
(Written 2005)

DeLores Richards

From the throne of God is a riv-er of life. Fr-om E-den it

flows, heaven-ly gar-den of God. And it wat-ers the tree of

e-tern-al life. And as cry-stal it flows, heaven-ly gar den of

God. I'm walk-ing in the gar-den that God made for me. I'm

touch-ing the tree of e-tern-i-ty. He plant-ed it there just for

you and for me. To this ci-ty we come heaven-ly gar den of God.

HIS HAND IS LEADING ME

1977 I thought that God was out there. By 2005 I had grown in my spiritual life to discover that His hand was indeed guiding my every move. We call the picture above a hand. It is doing God's work. And--- what does the hand of God look like? This is still a vague picture to us all and it is doubtful that anyone can completely explain this to us. Someday we will know.

HIS HAND IS LEADING ME
(Written 2005)

DeLores Richards

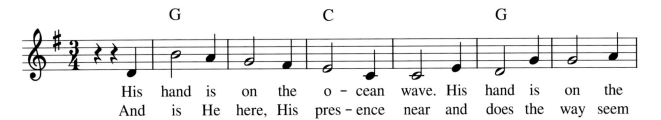

His hand is on the o - cean wave. His hand is on the
And is He here, His pres - ence near and does the way seem

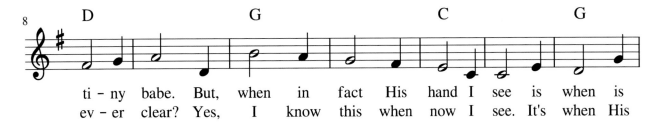

ti - ny babe. But, when in fact His hand I see is when is
ev - er clear? Yes, I know this when now I see. It's when His

hand is lead - ing me.
hand is lead - ing me. He heals my mind, He heals my heart. My

spir-it is new right from the start. He gives me grace each day I

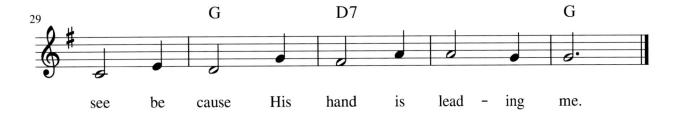

see be cause His hand is lead - ing me.

TOGETHERNESS CAN BE A PRAYER

In 2006, we renewed our vows after 50 years of marriage and music. The Lord put together a life for us that we did not expect. We can be thankful that instead of going down a path that we selected, we accepted one less traveled. This song indicates our dedication to the concept that togetherness will bring happiness into a marriage. It can be a prayer to lead us on through life.

TOGETHERNESS CAN BE A PRAYER
(Written 9/24/2006- 50 Years) DeLores Richards

Fif - ty years of mem - o - ries are like a - fleet - ing song. The
Re - memb - er all those new - born souls that came to our life. The

years have come and gone from us but we're for - ev - er young. The
way they brought us tears of joy, the way they brought us strife. And

years were fire and they were ice, but I would not change a thing. I
thru it all to - get - her ness was there to light our way. It

feel that God was on the road that we both trav - eled on. We re-joyce in to-
brought us thru the good and bad and con quered ev - ery day.

get - her-ness that brought us where we are. He fol - lowed ev - ery step we took. We

fol-lowed-ev - ery star. And if to-get-her - ness can be a prayer to lead us on, I

pledge my love to you a - new as we

walk in - to the sun.

ANGELS ARE ALWAYS THERE

In 1921, a little scared girl walked the planks from a houseboat. Tiny as she was, she already knew that the angels were her protectors in this world. She would skip along, as kids do, balancing on imaginary thoughts and dreams, getting through her daily schedule.

Mother was raised on the Columbia River in houseboats. Her dad fished as did many of her relatives. Her playmates were her four brothers. She was often sent out to work in other homes and to live there. Her folks were spiritualists. She learned about Jesus in one of the homes she stayed in, and from that time, this memory was prominent in her life. She felt the need to know more and she had her calling to be baptized in 1962 and to give her life to Jesus.

Mom was born in 1914. In 2008, my mother passed on. She was almost.

94 years old. I reflect on her life. She wrote some things that I remember well. One particular thing she mentioned was that she left us in the care of angels that "were always there."

She taught us to be the very best we could be and accomplish much throughout our lives. We have done this. Her education was not much, but she brought herself up from her humble beginning. She wrote these words which I made into a song. I expanded her advice to include her own life. (Photograph by Gavin Allanwood)

ANGELS ARE ALWAYS THERE
Written in 2008

DeLores Richards

On the fifth day of No vem ber in nine teen twen ty
The years went by. She went to school. It was like a
Time went by so quick - ly and she raised a fam - i -
She wrote these words to guide us when she turned nine ty

one, a house boat sits by a tall old wil low tree.
chore. Four big broth ers at play, girls were such a bore.
ly. She taught both of her girls ve - ry ve - ry well.
three. I treas - ure now in ev ry thing I do.

On a slip - ry plank on the riv - er, a
She had no shoes. She had one dress. The
She knew ang - els would be their shin - ing light
As the things of life are way too much, I

child walks to the shore. She has no fear 'cause she can see the
teach - er was so nice. She had those shoes and the ang - els did
for ev - ery step. She left them in the ang - els hands to
hear her say to me, "When trou - bles are too diff - i - cult to

ang - els. She knew the ang - els were al ways with her. there.
work twice. She knew the ang - els were al - ways with her there.
lead them. She knew the ang - els were al - ways with them there.
bear, then re - mem - ber ang - els are al ways with you there."

WE HEAR YOU. AMERICA HEARS YOU!

I've always wanted to write a great patriotic song. This is my attempt.

"We hear you" is taken from a speech which President George Bush gave when the two towers were destroyed in 2001 on 9/11. It touched my heart. "I can hear you and the rest of the world hears you," he said. During the years of President Trump, another theme came out which I had already written into this song a few years before— "Greater than ever before."

The statue of Liberty stands tall despite the unrest today in the country. She fights the clouds that surround her. I conclude that we are still a great country. We are a shining light on a hill—a beacon of freedom. Share this with me!   (Photograph Julius Drost)

WE HEAR YOU (AMERICA HEARS YOU)
(Written 2014)

President George Bush 2001-9/11

DeLores Richards

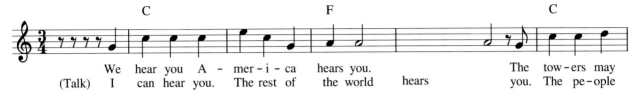

We hear you A - mer - i - ca hears you. The tow-ers may
(Talk) I can hear you. The rest of the world hears you. The pe-ople

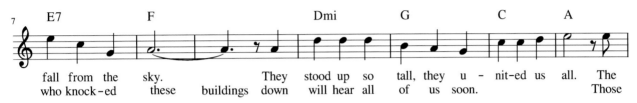

fall from the sky. They stood up so tall, they u - nit-ed us all. The
who knock-ed these buildings down will hear all of us soon. Those

pain that we suf-fered will not be in vain. A - mer-i-ca is strong-er. - A - mer-i-ca is
words that we hea - rd in - spired our re - birth. A - mer-i-ca is stong-er. - A - mer-i-ca is

strong-er. She's great-er than ev-er be - fore. We hear you. A - mer - i-ca hears you. She's
strong-er. She's great-er than ev-er be - fore.

bet - ter than ev er be - fore. We all feel your pain. It u - nites us just the same. A - mer-i-ca is

strong-er. A mer - i-ca is strong-er. She's great - er than eve - er be -

fore.

BAMBI'S BOOGIE

So, now it is seventy years later then when my generation, the young people of the 1950's, brought in "the age of rock." It was our generation that brought in Elvis Presley. It was our generation that "rocked around the clock." It almost seems like I was not a participant. I was just an onlooker watching all the marvelous changes happening in our world. The teens danced, the drums beat, and we all changed the world of music. Our Parents were dismayed.

They named me "Bambi" when I was in the band because of my big brown eyes and "deer in the headlights look."

This is my boogie! It's not the ordinary chord change! So- if you are playing this, you had better be ready to go everywhere when it comes to chords on your keyboard or your strings.   HAVE FUN!   Antoine-Julien (photograph)

BAMBI'S BOOGIE

(Written 2016)

DeLores Richards

A PERFECT WORLD

Is this our perfect world? God made it perfect but left us with the responsibility of creating within it a perfect world for ourselves. He gives us the ground. We plant His seed. We work to make our yards more perfect. We share.
It is not a thing that stops. It is a life-long endeavor. (PHOTOGRAPH -ZANE LEE)

A PERFECT WORLD
(Written 2017)

DeLores Richards

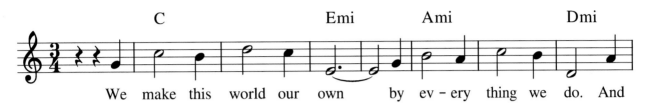

We make this world our own by ev - ery thing we do. And

that's the way we have a per-fect world. It's here from God a -

bove. He made it with his love. He left it up to us – A-per fect world.

Would you be will-ing to do your part and make it your

mis-sion to give it a start? It's here for you and me. It's all that

we can see. Guard it with your heart. a per-fect world.

JOIN IN LIFE TODAY

Here exists a problem. We do not know how to get from here to there! We do not know how to obtain the water of life!

Our minds are limited. When we think of water, we see water only. When we think of flying, we see birds or a plane or something about which we have physical knowledge. God has his own language, but it seems hidden from us completely. He speaks about what we know but thinks in greater terms. WE CAN ONLY WAIT TO FIND OUT THESE SECRETS!

JOIN IN LIFE TODAY
(Written 2017)

DeLores Richards

Join in life to - day. Take me to the sky Call me as you would.
Fly us up to heav'n, No lim - it is there. Ev - ery where I see

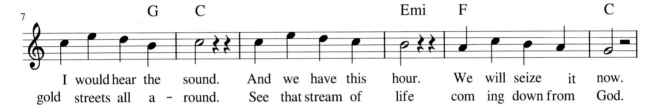

I would hear the sound. And we have this hour. We will seize it now.
gold streets all a - round. See that stream of life com ing down from God.

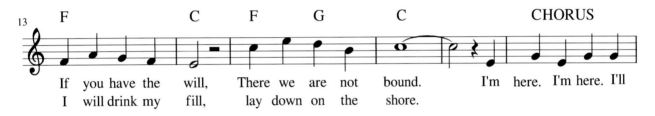

If you have the will, There we are not bound. I'm here. I'm here. I'll
I will drink my fill, lay down on the shore.

al ways be. I'll nev-er leave it now. We will shine up - on that sil - ver high - way. Fly

with me to the hea vens. Fly with me to the heav-ens and Join with me in life to -

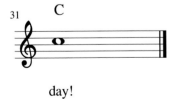

day!

A WALK INTO THE WOODLANDS

By Diana Richards Gulley

A WALK INTO THE WOODLANDS
(Written December 2019)

DeLores Richards

JANUARY 2020

January is always full of promise. We see backwards a few years to compare, but we cannot see what is in store. God is eternal. We are not.

2020 started out as a new beginning, a wonderful number. Now as we come to the end of a rather difficult year, we see that it was not what we expected. The economy went underground. We suffered because of Covid-19. Our country and people faced riots and division. Crimes increased. Families were torn apart. Small business was lost. Mental health and suicide was a major issue. Churches closed.

There was division and a lack of unity to accept a tragic part of history.

But, by the end of 2020, we could see that our people became strong in the quest to learn to cope.

AND COPE THEY DID! We welcome 2121 !

JANUARY 2020

DeLores Richards

ON THE ICE

At the start of the year, I named this instrumental "On the ice." WHY? This time of year is normally cold and unpleasant. The snow and ice are pretty. However, we soon become tired of it. In a way, this song looks forward to how we would all-- in a short time—be approaching 2020 as a time to try to climb out of the covid-19 mess— much as we dig in our boots out of a snowbank.

ON THE ICE

JANUARY-DECEMBER 2020

DeLores May Richards

PIANO FANASTY SCHOTTISCHE

This old 1800's piano has had a place of honor in our house since the 1960's when our oldest began to take her first piano lessons.

It takes me back to about 1950 when my sister and I attended folk dances at a local grange hall. They were organized by my stepdad's sister, Aunt Vi.

The schottische was one of the favored dances, along with the bunny hop and others. We would spin around the hall, feet moving to the tempo of the music. A square dance or two would keep the excitement going for the evening. Often I have wished for the energy we had then as kids to be able to do this again. That was 70 years ago. Now I write music and my fingers can do the dancing. This is my special schottische.

PIANO FANTASY SCHOTTISCHE
Written February 8, 2020

DeLores Richards

In Loving Memory

June G. Harkcom

June 30, 1914 — May 2, 2008

A BIT OF IRELAND
(Written March 2020)

DeLores Richards

HEATHER ON THE HILLS OF IRELAND

(PHOTOGRAPH BY SEAN PAUL KENNEAR)

Could anything be as beautiful as a field of Heather? When writing my last song "A bit of Ireland," I viewed information about Ireland on my computer. I saw hills of Heather. I can see why the Irish settled so much in the Pacific Northwest. They saw here a bit of Ireland in the fields of green. I wrote an instrumental about Heather and some day I will go for myself and see these fields. For now, this is what I see---a picture taken in the United Kingdom.

HEATHER ON THE HILLS OF IRELAND
(Written February 2020)

DeLores Richards

ON THE MOVE

March was a month when everyone was still enjoying events. We were traveling anywhere we wanted to go. We think that we got Covid-19 at a bluegrass festival in Bellevue, Washington. From then on everything came to a complete halt like a bad accident on one of our freeways—or maybe all of them. We made a list of everything we had to do at our house and STAYED HOME!

ON THE MOVE
(Written March 2020)

DeLores Richards

ALL IS DONE

This is a song in dedication to all the working couples that are separated due to work time hours.

Work is necessary but—it's not the main thing in life. We need to take time evaluating our priorities so that life is balanced. This is a picture of one such couple.

Our daughter, Lori Ann and Dale, married during a cruise just as the pandemic began.

Music in their hearts

ALL IS DONE (Written March 2020)

DeLores Richards

LAUGHING AT THE RAIN

The thing about Oregon state is that sometimes you make plans and all at once it is raining. It may rain for days or just minutes. No one can ever predict the Oregon weather. So, you plan and adapt to whatever comes along.

So, in March, the rain is a little warmer. When summer comes, it is downright pleasant.

THE RAIN IS COMING!

LAUGHING AT THE RAIN

March 2020

DeLores Richards

DO YOU HEAR THE SUNSHINE?

So many kinds of birds. They know that God cares for them. They look forward to each morning. It seems to me that sometimes they have a greater appreciation of the sunshine. Sometimes we do not use our five senses to determine what are the beautiful things in this world. Just looking at the birds above shows us that they understand the sunshine is more than just sight. They can feel, hear and even touch the sky above them to bring to themselves the full benefit of the sun. Should we do less?

DO YOU HEAR THE SUNSHINE ?
Written April 2020

DeLores Richards

FIELDS OF CLOVER FLOWING OVER

Covid-19 is now a motivation for writing more songs.

This is sort of a survival plan for our household. We can grab a guitar, strum away and sing from our hearts.

FIELDS OF LOVE FLOWING OVER

FIELDS OF CLOVER FLOWING OVER

(Written April 2020)

DeLores Richards

STAY AT HOME

In the middle of Covid-19, you see a lot of lonely people. We have not had this because we have each other. It is important to be able to share. And, we have had social distancing with our family picnics.

The matter of being lonely is wide-spread. It covers the whole country. You will see depression where it has never been before. Where you have a family, you might see domestic disturbances at a greater rate. People want to work. They want to go to school. They want to go out. They want things back to normal. So—we end up wondering "WHAT IS NORMAL?"

STAY AT HOME

Written May 2020

DeLores Richards

Etude for Opening the world

You want to sing. You want to dance. You want to have a parade.

We thought we were thru with Covid-19. Now we know better. In May, we were all making plans for summer activities. We had big vacation thoughts. There would be events, family gatherings and lots of opportunities to play our music.

IT WAS NOT TO BE!

ETUDE FOR OPENING THE WORLD

Written May 2020

DeLores Richards

SUMMER SUN SONG

It is the same sun that shines on everyone. It is a uniting force even during Covid-19. We enjoyed the summer with social distancing. A time to admire God's beauty......a time to relax....and to catch up on things at home. And, back to Church and gatherings in our picnic area-- a new baby (great granddaughter) a new marriage for our daughter.

God thank you for your blessings!

SUMMER SUN SONG

(WRITTEN JULY2020)

DeLores Richards

TURNAROUND WINDOW

June 2020 was a time when stores opened. People were allowed out more to visit friends and relatives. The worse was over. We were   enjoying our new freedom. But—in July—the situation turned around. The testing showed that the rate of infection increased, and the states started closing again. Masks were required everywhere. Deaths went down but it was still with us--just waiting around the corner.

Our family enjoyed a reunion picnic on July 4, but another window was almost upon us where more precautions had to be taken. And--so we did our best to show our support and do our best under the circumstances.

One good thing, for two months straight, job creation numbers were up, and unemployment rates were down. Walmart, Home Depot, Amazon, and any such were booming. Small shops, restaurants, and tourist spots were going out of business at an alarming rate.

TURNAROUND WINDOW

JULY 2020

DeLores Richards

ALONE TOGETHER NOW

 At the end of august, Covid-19 had turned around considerably in our county in Oregon. Astoria was open partially. We still wore masks. We still avoided shopping unless we really needed groceries. We started a list at the beginning of the pandemic. We are almost to the end of the outside list. We painted. We built decks. We landscaped. We cleaned our basement and garage. If needed, we have an extended list for all the things we want to do inside. Painting, fixing, building there too. We went on one trip to Portland because the refrigerator that we needed could not be found in our locale—and our refrigerator had died. Everything is on back order. Astoria is isolated. That was our one trip out of town.

SETEMBER 2020 WILL BE OUR 64TH ANNIVERSARY.

ALONE TOGETHER NOW

Written August 2020

DeLores Richards

I'VE GOT A NEW LOOK, A NEW OUTLOOK
Covid-19 gave everyone a chance to decide what
was important in their lives.

It was wonderful to arrange special times where
we could get together with our families.
July 4th, we had a special gathering with our
extended families complete with turkey--outside
in our picnic area. By November, COVID-19 was
everywhere. Some big family Thanksgiving events
were being canceled.

I'VE GOT A NEW LOOK

WRITTEN SEPTEMBER 2020

DeLores Richards

EARLY MORNING KISS AT THE WATER TOWER

Health-wise, be sure you get your exercise during

Covid-19. Routines are especially important during this time—and we have something to look forward to everyday. It is out there.

So, we need to get out there-Walk, sing, and play!

MORNING KISS AT THE WATER TOWER
WRITTEN DECEMBER 2020

DeLores Richards

MID COVID-19 DRAMA

The consequences of Covid-19 are as deep as the Grand Canyon that we visited last year. It's a hole that the nation is trying to climb out of, and it seems to be an impossible task. Restrictions are beyond sensible. We sacrifice our businesses, our families and our mental health and it seems like we are slipping backwards - unable to climb back to our normal world. Prices have gone up, shortages are prevalent. However, here at the end of the year, we have the vaccine that we have been waiting for. Everyone, get a grip on the slope and make that awaited CLIMB OUT.

MID COVID-19 DRAMA

WRITTEN -MARCH-DECEMBER 2020   DeLores Richards

Sherry and Ronnie

David and Yvette,
Juliana and Thaddeus

Lori Ann and Dale

Diana and Glenn

OUR FAMILY

KEEP ON SMILING.

KEEP ON PLUCKING ON YOUR HEARTSTRINGS.

BYE FOR NOW!

Made in the USA
Coppell, TX
25 April 2021